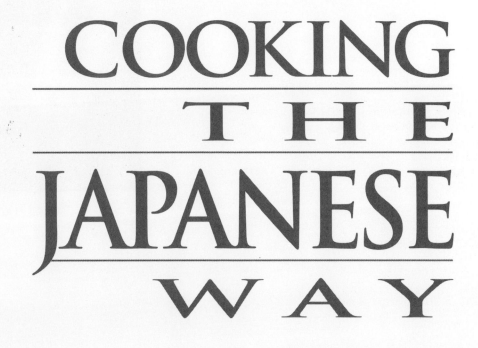

COOKING THE JAPANESE WAY

Lerner Publications Company
A division of Lerner Publishing Group
241 First Avenue North
Minneapolis, MN 55401 U.S.A.

Website address: www.lernerbooks.com

Library of Congress Cataloging-in-Publication Data

Weston, Reiko.
    Cooking the Japanese way / by Reiko Weston.—Rev. & expanded.
        p.   cm. — (Easy menu ethnic cookbooks)
    Includes index.
    ISBN 0-8225-4114-9 (lib. bdg. : alk. paper)
    1. Cookery, Japanese—Juvenile literature. 2. Japan—Social life and customs—Juvenile literature. [1. Cookery, Japanese. 2. Japan—Social life and customs.] I. Title.
II. Series.
TX724.5.J3 W47 2002
641.5952—dc21   00-009537

Manufactured in the United States of America
1 2 3 4 5 6 – JR – 07 06 05 04 03 02

easy menu ethnic cookbooks

COOKING

revised and expanded

THE

to include new low-fat

JAPANESE

and vegetarian recipes

WAY

Reiko Weston

Lerner Publications Company • Minneapolis

Contents

Introduction

Japan is known around the world as a producer of efficient, well-made automobiles, televisions, cameras, computers, and thousands of other useful machines and gadgets. Although Japanese technology is famous, other aspects of Japanese life may not be as well known to people in other parts of the world. Japan is also a country proud of its ancient cultural traditions. A distinctive style of cooking is one very important tradition that lives on in modern Japan.

Like the cuisine of other countries with long histories, Japanese cooking has grown and changed over more than 2,000 years. Important developments in Japanese history, such as the first contact with Europeans in the 1500s, brought new foods and new cooking methods into Japanese life. Despite these changes, the basic elements of Japanese cooking have remained the same for a very long time.

Chirashi-zushi, or "scattered" sushi rice (recipe on page 66), is a colorful dish traditionally served on Girls' Day.

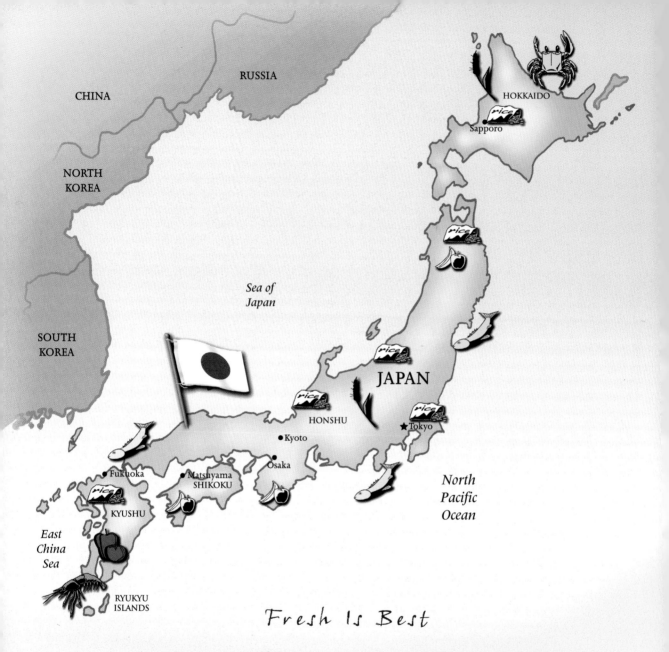

Fresh Is Best

As in the past, one of the most important characteristics of modern Japanese cooking is that it uses only the freshest kinds of foods. Japanese cooks usually shop every day, buying food to be prepared for that day's meals. This emphasis on fresh food is part of the deep respect for nature that is so important in Japanese culture. The

Japanese believe that the products of the earth and the sea should be used in ways that preserve their natural forms and flavors as much as possible.

When they plan meals during the year, Japanese cooks try to use the fruits and vegetables that grow in that particular season. In spring, wild plants such as *warabi* (fern shoots) and *seri* (Japanese parsley) can be gathered in woodlands and forests. Summer brings the ripening of such familiar garden vegetables as tomatoes, lettuce, cucumbers, eggplants, beans, and peas. In the autumn, a wild mushroom harvest takes place when the large *matsutake* appears in pine forests. Winter meals feature root vegetables such as carrots and turnips as well as daikon, a large white radish, and the root of the burdock, a plant viewed as a weed in the United States.

At any time of the year, Japanese cooks can buy fresh fish caught in the waters that surround the island nation. Fish markets display tuna, sea bass, yellowtail, and cod along with other products of the sea such as octopus, sea urchins, and many delicious kinds of edible seaweed. Excellent beef, pork, and chicken are also available and appear on Japanese menus.

Cooking the Japanese Way

When they prepare food, the Japanese use basic cooking methods that preserve or enhance the natural flavors of all the ingredients. Most of these methods are simple and easy, but they produce dishes that taste delicious and look beautiful.

One of the most common styles of Japanese cooking is called *nimono*. This category includes dishes that are made by gently boiling or simmering ingredients such as fish, meat, or vegetables in a seasoned broth. *Yakimono* is food prepared by broiling, usually over a charcoal fire. The famous Japanese *tempura*—food that has been deep-fried in batter—belongs to the general group of *agemono*, or fried things.

A special category of Japanese cooking is *nabemono*, hearty one-pot dishes that are usually cooked at the table and include meat, fish, vegetables, tofu, and sometimes noodles. *Aemono* dishes are made up of cooked vegetables and seafood that are served cold and tossed with various sauces—*sunomono* dishes have vinegar dressings; *ohitashi* are boiled green vegetables topped with *katsuobushi* (dried bonito fish shavings) or sesame seeds and served with soy sauce. *Tsukemono* are the many pickled vegetables that are served with most Japanese meals.

When Japanese cooks plan the day's meals, they choose different dishes from these and other basic cooking categories. Japanese breakfasts, lunches, and dinners all consist of foods prepared in different ways or with contrasting flavors. A sharp-tasting sunomono dish might be served with *teriyaki*, a broiled food with a sweet sauce. Crunchy tsukemono makes a good contrast to a nabemono brimming with meat or seafood and vegetables. Unlike Western cooks— who plan certain types of foods for each of the day's main meals— Japanese cooks mix and match foods. Soup, for example, is as likely to appear at breakfast as at lunch.

The recipes in this book are divided into groups based on the style of cooking or preparation they require. You will be able to plan meals in the Japanese style by choosing dishes from these basic categories.

When choosing and preparing dishes for a meal, Japanese cooks think not only of the food's freshness and flavor but also of its appearance. They believe that good food should appeal to the mind and the eye as well as to the taste buds. Therefore, they try to make sure that the colors of the various ingredients and dishes in a meal look pleasing together. Many cooks use special methods of cutting and arranging ingredients. Finally, they serve food in well designed bowls, plates, and cups that make an appropriate background for its color and texture.

In Japan, cooking and serving food is considered an art. But it is an art that is an essential part of everyday life. Japanese cooks preparing

Many sushi shops offer appealing displays as a way to advertise their goods and to attract customers.

meals for their families rely on the same principles of freshness, simplicity, and beauty as do chefs in the finest restaurants. When you try the recipes in this book, think of yourself as an artist using vegetables, fish, and meat to make something that is both delicious and beautiful. Then you will really be cooking the Japanese way.

Eating with chopsticks means that table manners in Japan are different from those in countries where flatware is used. For example, it is good manners to pick up a rice bowl and hold it so that the food doesn't fall from the chopsticks to the table or into your lap. It is impolite, however, to use the "eating" ends of your chopsticks to help yourself from a nabemono pot. Instead, you should turn the chopsticks around to use the "clean" ends for dishing up. Sometimes special serving chopsticks are provided.

Though chopsticks may seem tricky at first, they are not difficult to manage once you have learned the basic technique. The key to using them is to hold the inside stick still while moving the outside stick back and forth. The pair then act as pincers to pick up pieces of food.

Hold the thicker end of the first chopstick in the crook of your thumb, resting the lower part lightly against the inside of your ring finger. Then put the second chopstick between the tips of your index and middle fingers and hold it with your thumb, much as you would hold a pencil. Now you can make the outer chopstick move by bending your index and middle fingers toward the inside chopstick. The tips of the two sticks should come together like pincers when you bend your fingers. Once you get a feel for the technique, just keep practicing. Soon you'll be an expert!

Japanese children start using chopsticks at an early age.

Japanese Kabuki players perform a New Year's play on the beach at sunrise to welcome the new year.

Holidays and Festivals

Holidays and festivals of all kinds are an important part of Japanese culture. Just as Japanese people admire beauty in everyday activities, they also love to celebrate special occasions with beautiful and colorful festivities. Japan observes national holidays, when most offices, shops, and schools are closed, as well as many other festivals and events throughout the year. Most events have their origins in either Shintoism or Buddhism, Japan's two main religions. However, they are widely observed by people of diverse spiritual beliefs and practices. For most Japanese people, holidays are a time to have fun with friends and family—and, of course, to enjoy all kinds of delicious foods!

The most important time of year in Japan is Oshogatsu, or New Year's. Oshogatsu is a whole season, not just one day. January 1–3 are national holidays, but the festivities start before December 31 and may last until January 15, or even longer.

To get off to a perfect start, people prepare for the coming year by paying debts, finishing up business, and generally getting everything shipshape. Many people and businesses throw *bonenkai*, parties that help everyone forget the troubles of the old year and look forward to the joys of the new. People also clean their houses or apartments thoroughly, and almost every home's doorway is festooned with *kadomatsu*, an arrangement of pine boughs, bamboo, and plum blossoms. Some people even attach small kadomatsu to their cars! This decoration represents strength and character and is intended to attract good fortune and good spirits. People also hang *shimenawa*, ropes of rice straw, near the entrances to their homes for protection against evil spirits.

According to Shinto beliefs, the *toshigami*, or god of the new year, visits Japanese households during the New Year's season. To welcome this special guest, families set out *kagamimochi* in the main rooms of their homes. Kagamimochi are decorations made of two round *mochi*, rice cakes made from glutinous (sticky) rice that has been pounded, flattened, and cut into various shapes. One rice cake is stacked on top of a larger one and decorated with items such as dried persimmons, fern leaves, and seaweed. On January 11, families remove the kagamimochi from its special stand and the bottom rice cake is cut and eaten for good luck.

To give cooks a break during the first days of the new year, special foods called *osechi* are prepared ahead of time. Osechi are served in beautifully decorated boxes called *jubako*. Jubako have three or more stacked shelves, each filled with food. Dozens of different goodies might be inside, but a few common ones are herring roe (eggs), dried sardines, and stewed black beans. Most osechi have special meaning. For example, herring roe symbolizes fertility, and stewed black soybeans symbolize good health. Traditionally, these foods were made at home, but in modern times many families buy them already prepared and packaged.

On Omisoka, New Year's Eve, many people eat *toshikoshi soba*, or "year-crossing noodles." Eating this soup with its extra-long, thin noodles as the new year begins is supposed to ensure a long life. At midnight, Buddhist temples ring bells or gongs 108 times, symbolically getting rid of people's cares and worries.

On New Year's morning, families put on their best clothes and gather to toast the new year with a drink of *otoso*—spiced *sake*, or rice wine. Many people make their first visits of the year to shrines and temples. At home, they enjoy a delicious breakfast of *ozoni*, a traditional New Year's soup. The rest of New Year's Day is spent relaxing, playing games, and eating.

Other customary foods throughout the New Year's season are baked chestnuts, rice dumplings, omelets, sweet potatoes, and rice porridge. Families continue to enjoy these tasty treats as the holiday season winds down and things get back to normal.

Another big holiday in Japan is Kodomo no Hi, or Children's Day, on May 5. Originally, May 5 was Tango no Sekku, Boys' Day, and March 3 was Hina Matsuri, Girls' Day. In 1948 May 5 was declared a national holiday to honor all children and to make good wishes for their futures. However, special Boys' Day traditions are also still practiced on this day, and Girls' Day is still observed on March 3.

To celebrate the sons of the family on Boys' Day, Japanese fathers set up bamboo poles outside their homes and fly *koi nobori*, colorful

Colorful carp wind socks flutter in celebration of Boys' Day.

wind socks in the shape of carp. Each boy has his own koi nobori, the largest for the oldest son and the smallest for the youngest. Because the carp swims upstream, battling against the current, this spirited fish is a symbol of strength and perseverance. Inside the house, families set up displays of warrior dolls, swords, helmets, and other items associated with the courageous samurai warriors. Boys and their friends and family munch on special treats of kashiwamochi, rice cakes filled with bean paste and wrapped in oak leaves, and chimaki, rice dumplings wrapped in bamboo leaves.

On Girls' Day, also called the Dolls' Festival, girls enjoy special attention. Households with daughters display sets of dolls just for this occasion. These dolls have usually been passed down from mothers to daughters and are highly treasured. A set may include only two dolls, representing the emperor and empress of Japan. More elaborate sets contain figures of the royal servants and members of the court, doll-sized furniture, dishes—sometimes complete with tiny food—lanterns, and other accessories. Fresh peach blossoms, symbols of beauty, decorate the display stand. Japanese girls dress in their nicest kimonos and invite friends to visit, share tea and snacks, and admire the dolls. Traditional foods at the tea parties are hishimochi (pink and green diamond-shaped rice cakes), sweet rice crackers, and sushi rice. A special kind of sweet, mild sake, is also drunk.

In addition to national holidays, Japanese families celebrate many festivals, or matsuri. The largest of these is Obon, the Buddhist festival of the dead. Obon is usually held August 13 through August 15 or 16, although it sometimes takes place in the middle of July. The date varies according to whether the lunar or the solar calendar is used.

Based on the belief that spirits of the dead come back to earth for a visit during this time of the year, Obon is like a great party to welcome these spirits. Families try to be together for this event, during which they remember and honor their ancestors. Before the festival begins, people visit family graves to tidy them, decorate them with

Three girls dance during the festival of Obon.

flowers and greenery, and prepare them for the spirits' arrival. Most families also make offerings of fruit, rice, incense, and other pleasant gifts, both at the gravesite and at the household altar.

On the first night of the festival, Japanese families go to local graveyards. As night falls, they light lanterns and carry them home, hanging them outside the door to guide the spirits. They may also light a welcoming bonfire, called *mukaebi*. Then the family shares a festive meal, which always includes the favorite foods of departed ancestors.

During the days of the festival, nearly every town and city celebrates with *bon-odori*, traditional rhythmic dances accompanied by folk singing and the *taiko* drum. The taiko drummer stands on a *yagura*, a high platform or tower set up in the main square or park and decorated with brightly colored lanterns. People of all ages perform the dance in a circle around the yagura. The exact steps of the dance vary from town to town and region to region. But in all parts of Japan this is a joyful event, and many members of the community join in the celebration. In larger towns, there may also be stands selling gifts, good-luck charms, and tasty treats to onlookers and participants alike.

On the final night of Obon, it is time to guide the spirits back to their world. Many cooks prepare snacks for the spirits to take with them on their journey. Once again, lanterns and bonfires light the way. Finally, people gather by lakes, rivers, and coasts to launch the spirits in small boats carrying miniature lanterns. The names of the people being remembered are usually written on the boat or on little pieces of paper in the boat. These tiny crafts are set into the water, and families bid farewell to the spirits of their ancestors until next Obon.

Many Japanese festivals are based on the seasons. *Setsubun*, meaning "dividing of the seasons," takes place around February 3 to celebrate the beginning of spring according to the lunar calendar. The main activity of this festival is *mamemaki*, or bean-throwing. As part of an ancient custom, roasted soybeans are thrown outside the home to keep demons out and thrown inside to attract good fortune. This ritual is often performed by the head of the family, but children usually join in the fun, sometimes wearing scary masks. As they scatter the beans they chant, *"Oni wa soto! Fuku wa uchi!"* meaning, "Devils out! Happiness in!" Afterward, it is considered good luck to pick up and eat one soybean for each year in one's life, plus one more for the coming year. Temples and shrines hold public mamemaki ceremonies, often featuring actors, sumo wrestlers, and other celebrities.

In early February, Sapporo's week-long Snow Festival, Yuki Matsuri, draws visitors from all over the world. Located on Hokkaido, Japan's northernmost island, Sapporo has the perfect chilly climate for this event. The festival began in 1950 when a group of high school students created six large snow sculptures. These days, hundreds of sculptures are created each year from more than 30,000 tons of snow. Families stroll Sapporo's main park and streets admiring the giant sculptures of people, buildings, cartoon characters, and animals, many of which are lit at night. Children, bundled up in their warmest clothes, enjoy whizzing down ice slides. Afterward, they visit a shop for steaming bowls of *ramen*, a noodle soup that is Sapporo's specialty.

A warmer celebration takes place in April, when Japan's many cherry trees begin to bloom. Sakura Matsuri, or the Cherry-Blossom Festival, is especially popular in the bustling capital city of Tokyo, where families, schoolchildren, and businesspeople relax in the parks to enjoy picnics and to admire the beautiful blossoms. In rural areas, the big event of spring or early summer is rice planting. Held May through July according to region, rice-planting festivals offer prayers for a good harvest. They feature music, dancing, parades, and ceremonies during which girls and women plant rice seedlings.

Hundreds of other matsuri take place around Japan throughout the year. Whether they celebrate nature, honor the past, or look forward to the future, Japanese holidays and festivals are bright, colorful events that always include lots of fun and plenty of wonderful food.

Before You Begin

Japanese cooking calls for some ingredients that you may not know. Sometimes special cookware is also used, although the recipes in this book can easily be prepared with ordinary utensils and pans.

The most important thing you need to know before you start is how to be a careful cook. On the following page, you'll find a few rules that will make your cooking experience safe, fun, and easy. Next, take a look at the "dictionary" of terms and special ingredients. You may also want to read the list of tips on preparing healthy, low-fat meals.

Once you've picked out a recipe to try, read through it from beginning to end. Now you are ready to shop for ingredients and to organize the cookware you will need. When you have assembled everything, you're ready to begin cooking.

A simple miso ramen soup (recipe on page 68) can be dressed up with chicken, spinach, mushrooms, and more. Be creative!

The Careful Cook

Whenever you cook, there are certain safety rules you must always keep in mind. Even experienced cooks follow these rules when they are in the kitchen.

- Always wash your hands before handling food. Thoroughly wash all raw vegetables and fruits to remove dirt, chemicals, and insecticides. Wash uncooked poultry, fish, and meat under cold water.
- Use a cutting board when cutting up vegetables and fruits. Don't cut them up in your hand! And be sure to cut in a direction *away* from you and your fingers.
- Long hair or loose clothing can easily catch fire if brought near the burners of a stove. If you have long hair, tie it back before you start cooking.
- Turn all pot handles toward the back of the stove so that you will not catch your sleeves or jewelry on them. This is especially important when younger brothers and sisters are around. They could easily knock off a pot and get burned.
- Always use a pot holder to steady hot pots or to take pans out of the oven. Don't use a wet cloth on a hot pan because the steam it produces could burn you.
- Lift the lid of a steaming pot with the opening away from you so that you will not get burned.
- If you get burned, hold the burn under cold running water. Do not put grease or butter on it. Cold water helps to take the heat out, but grease or butter will only keep it in.
- If grease or cooking oil catches fire, throw baking soda or salt at the bottom of the flame to put it out. (Water will *not* put out a grease fire.) Call for help, and try to turn all the stove burners to "off."

Cooking Utensils

charcoal grill—A cooker in which charcoal provides the source of heat and food is placed on a grill above the coals

colander—A bowl-shaped dish with holes in it that is used for washing or draining food

sieve—A hand-held device with very small holes or fine netting that is used for draining or washing food

skewer—A thin stick used to hold small pieces of meat, fish, or vegetables for broiling or grilling. The Japanese use bamboo sticks as skewers.

steamer—A cooking utensil designed for cooking food with steam. Japanese steamers have tight-fitting lids and grates or racks for holding the food. In Western cooking, vegetables are often steamed in a basket that fits inside a saucepan.

Cooking Terms

baste—To pour or spoon liquid over food to flavor and moisten it as it cooks

boil—To heat a liquid over high heat until bubbles form and rise rapidly to the surface

bone—To remove the bones from meat or fish

broil—To cook directly under a heat source so that the side of the food facing the heat cooks rapidly

brown—To cook food quickly in fat over high heat so that the surface turns an even brown

dice—To chop food into small, square pieces

fold—To blend an ingredient with other ingredients by using a gentle overturning circular motion instead of by stirring or beating

grate—To cut into tiny pieces by rubbing the food against a grater; to shred

marinate—To soak food in a liquid to add flavor and to tenderize it

preheat—To allow an oven to warm up to a certain temperature before putting food in it

sauté—To fry quickly over high heat in oil or fat, stirring or turning the food to prevent burning

simmer—To cook over low heat in liquid kept just below its boiling point. Bubbles may occasionally rise to the surface.

Special Ingredients

bamboo shoots—Tender, fleshy yellow sprouts from bamboo canes. They can be bought fresh in Japan, and canned ones are usually available elsewhere.

chives—A member of the onion family whose thin, green stalks are chopped and used to garnish many dishes

dashinomoto—An instant powdered soup base made from dried seaweed and flakes of dried *bonito* fish called *katsuobushi*. (Homemade soup stock is called *dashi*.)

ginger root—A knobby, light brown root used to flavor food. To use fresh ginger root, slice off the amount called for, peel off the skin with the side of a spoon, and grate the flesh. Freeze the rest of the root for future use. Fresh ginger has a very zippy taste, so use it sparingly. (Don't substitute dried ground ginger in a recipe calling for fresh ginger, as the taste is very different.)

katsuobushi—Dried shavings of the bonito fish; used as a garnish for many dishes and to flavor soup stock

miso—A paste made from soybeans and used in soups, sauces, and as a garnish

noodles—An important staple that is available in many forms and served in many ways. Three popular kinds are *soba* (buckwheat noodles), *somen* (thin wheat noodles), and *udon* (thick wheat noodles).

rice—An important cereal grain that comes in three varieties. Short-grain rice, the kind used in the recipes in this book, has short, thick grains that tend to stick together when cooked. Sweet or glutinous rice is used to make special dishes. Long-grain rice is fluffy and absorbs more water than other types. It is not used in Japanese cooking.

rice vinegar—Vinegar made from rice

scallion—A variety of green onion

sesame seeds—Seeds from an herb grown in tropical countries. Sesame seeds are white or black in color and are often toasted and used either whole or crushed.

shiitake—Black mushrooms, either dried or fresh, used in Japanese cooking. Dried mushrooms must be rinsed in lukewarm water before cooking to make them tender.

shirataki—Yam noodles, available canned at most large supermarkets and at specialty food shops

soy sauce—A sauce made from soybeans and other ingredients that is used to flavor Asian cooking. Japanese soy sauce (*shoyu*) is recommended for the recipes in this book.

tofu—A processed curd made from soybeans

Healthy and Low-Fat Cooking Tips

Many modern cooks are concerned about preparing healthy, low-fat meals. Fortunately, Japanese food, with its use of fish and fresh produce, is already very low in fat. However, here are a few general tips for adapting the recipes in this book to be even healthier. Throughout the cookbook, you'll also find specific suggestions for individual recipes—and don't worry, they'll still taste delicious!

Almost all Japanese cooking uses soy sauce, a seasoning that, like salt, adds a great deal of flavor but is high in sodium. To lower the sodium content of these dishes, you may simply reduce the amount of soy sauce that you use. You can also substitute low-sodium soy sauce. Be aware that soy sauce labeled "light" is usually actually lighter in color than regular soy sauce, not lower in sodium.

Many Japanese dishes include meat or fish. However, it is easy to adapt most of the recipes in this book to be vegetarian. Tofu, already a common ingredient in Japanese dishes, is a simple and satisfying substitution for meat. Or try adding extra vegetables, especially hearty vegetables like mushrooms, sweet potatoes, or eggplant. In soups that call for dashinomoto, which contains fish shavings, you may substitute *konbu*, dried kelp.

A few recipes use vegetable oil for sautéing or omelet making. Reducing the amount of oil you use is one quick way to reduce fat. You can also substitute a low-fat or nonfat cooking spray for oil. It's a good idea to use a small, nonstick frying pan if you decide to use less oil than a recipe calls for.

There are many ways to prepare meals that are good for you and still taste great. As you become a more experienced cook, try experimenting with recipes and substitutions to find the methods that work best for you.

METRIC CONVERSIONS

Cooks in the United States measure both liquid and solid ingredients using standard containers based on the 8-ounce cup and the tablespoon. These measurements are based on volume, while the metric system of measurement is based on both weight (for solids) and volume (for liquids). To convert from U.S. fluid tablespoons, ounces, quarts, and so forth to metric liters is a straightforward conversion, using the chart below. However, since solids have different weights—one cup of rice does not weigh the same as one cup of grated cheese, for example—many cooks who use the metric system have kitchen scales to weigh different ingredients. The chart below will give you a good starting point for basic conversions to the metric system.

MASS (weight)

1 ounce (oz.)	=	28.0 grams (g)
8 ounces	=	227.0 grams
1 pound (lb.) or 16 ounces	=	0.45 kilograms (kg)
2.2 pounds	=	1.0 kilogram

LIQUID VOLUME

1 teaspoon (tsp.)	=	5.0 milliliters (ml)
1 tablespoon (tbsp.)	=	15.0 milliliters
1 fluid ounce (oz.)	=	30.0 milliliters
1 cup (c.)	=	240 milliliters
1 pint (pt.)	=	480 milliliters
1 quart (qt.)	=	0.95 liters (l)
1 gallon (gal.)	=	3.80 liters

LENGTH

¼ inch (in.)	=	0.6 centimeters (cm)
½ inch	=	1.25 centimeters
1 inch	=	2.5 centimeters

TEMPERATURE

212°F	=	100°C (boiling point of water)
225°F	=	110°C
250°F	=	120°C
275°F	=	135°C
300°F	=	150°C
325°F	=	160°C
350°F	=	180°C
375°F	=	190°C
400°F	=	200°C

(To convert temperature in Fahrenheit to Celsius, subtract 32 and multiply by .56)

PAN SIZES

8-inch cake pan	=	20 x 4-centimeter cake pan
9-inch cake pan	=	23 x 3.5-centimeter cake pan
11 x 7-inch baking pan	=	28 x 18-centimeter baking pan
13 x 9-inch baking pan	=	32.5 x 23-centimeter baking pan
9 x 5-inch loaf pan	=	23 x 13-centimeter loaf pan
2-quart casserole	=	2-liter casserole

A Japanese Table

A traditional Japanese table is about the height of a coffee table and is used for most dinners. On formal occasions, however, each diner eats off a small lacquer tray with legs. The Japanese do not use chairs. Diners kneel on large flat cushions called *zabuton*. Special guests are often seated before the *tokonoma*, or alcove, in which there is an arrangement of flowers, a decorative scroll, or some other art object.

Before the meal, each person is given a small, tightly rolled towel dampened with hot water. It is very refreshing and not considered impolite to bury your face in the towel before wiping your hands.

A Japanese table is set very simply. Large serving dishes are seldom used. Diners are served individual portions of food, each kind in its own separate china or lacquerware bowl. The bowls are chosen to complement the shape and color of the food.

Chopsticks (*hashi*) are the primary eating utensils except when *chawan mushi* is on the menu. Then diners use flat china spoons to eat this egg custard dish. Soup is drunk straight from the bowl after the vegetables and other pieces of food have been eaten with chopsticks.

Japanese diners gather for a meal around a traditional low table.

A Japanese Menu

Below is a sample Japanese menu for a typical day, along with shopping lists of necessary ingredients to prepare each of these three meals. Try these menus or come up with your own combinations. Remember that the only rule is to combine dishes that have different flavors and yet go well together.*

BREAKFAST

Bean paste soup

Rice

Tea

LUNCH

Cold noodles with dipping sauce

Sesame seed dressing with broccoli

Tea

SHOPPING LIST:
2 scallions
4 oz. tofu
short-grain white rice
dashinomoto
miso
loose green Japanese tea

SHOPPING LIST:
1 lb. broccoli
8 oz. soba, somen, or udon
    noodles
sesame seeds
Japanese soy sauce
dashinomoto
loose green Japanese tea
sugar

SUPPER

Broiled shrimp and
vegetables

Cucumber with crab

Rice

Tea

Fresh fruit

SHOPPING LIST:

1 green pepper
1 lb. whole mushrooms
2 cucumbers
fresh fruit such as plums,
   melon, apples, or
   tangerines
fresh ginger root
6 oz. crab, canned or frozen
1 lb. large shrimp, peeled
   and deveined, fresh or
   frozen
short-grain white rice
soy sauce
rice vinegar
loose green Japanese tea
sugar
salt

*If you plan to do a lot of Japanese cooking, you may
want to stock up on some basic ingredients. Rice, soy
sauce, dashinomoto, and fresh ginger all keep well and are
frequently called for in Japanese recipes. You may also
want to have a supply of loose green tea on hand.

Japanese Staples / Shushoku

No Japanese meal would be complete without small bowls of boiled or steamed rice to accompany the other dishes. In fact, the word for "rice"—*gohan*—is also the word for "food" in the Japanese language. Many Japanese families use electric rice cookers to be sure that this vital part of the meal is prepared perfectly every time.

Japanese people eat noodles almost as often as they eat rice, and they can choose from a great variety. Brown noodles called soba, made from buckwheat flour, are perhaps the most common. Udon and somen, two kinds of wheat-flour noodles, are also very popular. Noodles are even eaten for a quick snack in the way that an American might eat a sandwich or an apple.

Soybean products are another staple of the Japanese diet. It would be difficult to cook a Japanese meal without soy sauce, which is used as commonly as Westerners use salt. Two other soy products are miso, a soybean paste used in soups and other dishes, and tofu, a firm, custardlike substance made of soybean curd. Japanese cooks serve tofu by itself and also use it as an ingredient in many dishes. This unique soybean product is also popular in North America as a meatless source of protein.

A bowl of menrui, *or noodles, looks elegant when topped with cucumbers and mandarin orange slices. (Recipe on page 36.)*

Rice/ *Gohan*

Rice is the staple food in Japan, and a typical Japanese meal always includes hot, steamed rice. There are several different Japanese words that mean "rice," but the most dignified is gohan, or "honorable rice."

2 c. short-grain white rice, uncooked

2½ c. cold water

1. Wash rice in a pan with cold water and drain in a sieve.

2. In a covered heavy pot or saucepan, bring rice and 2½ c. water quickly to a boil. Lower heat and simmer until all water is absorbed (about 30 minutes).

3. Turn off heat and let rice steam itself for another 10 minutes.*

Preparation time: 10 minutes
Cooking time: 40 minutes
Serves 6 to 8

*For a simple but tasty variation of this recipe, just add 1 c. of cooked green peas at the end of Step 2 to make mame gohan, or rice with green peas.

Noodles / Menrui

In Japan, noodles are eaten hot or cold, and they are served in many different ways. Here are general instructions for cooking any kind of Japanese noodles—soba, somen, or udon—and recipes for serving them hot or cold.

8 oz. noodles, uncooked

1. Bring 6 c. of water to a boil. Add noodles and return water to a boil, stirring occasionally. Cook for about 20 minutes or until noodles are soft.

2. Drain noodles in a colander and rinse in cold water to stop the cooking process.

3. **For hot noodles:** set noodles aside and prepare broth.

4. **For cold noodles:** put noodles in refrigerator to cool while preparing the dipping sauce.

Cooking time: 20 to 30 minutes
Serves 4

Broth ingredients:

3 c. water

1 tbsp. dashinomoto*

4 tbsp. soy sauce

1 tbsp. sugar (or to taste)

chopped scallions or dried pepper flakes (optional)

1. Combine all broth ingredients in a pan and bring to a boil. Add noodles and bring to a boil again to heat noodles.

2. Remove from heat and serve noodles with broth in 4 individual bowls.

3. Top noodles with chopped scallions or dried red pepper flakes, if desired.

Preparation time: 10 minutes
Cooking time: 5 to 10 minutes

Dipping Sauce:

2 c. water

1 tsp. dashinomoto

6 tbsp. soy sauce

2 tsp. sugar (or to taste)

sliced cucumbers and canned
   mandarin oranges (optional)

1. Mix together all ingredients and pour into 4 small dishes for dipping.

2. Divide noodles among 4 bowls and garnish with sliced cucumber and mandarin oranges. Serve with dipping sauce.

Preparation time: 10 minutes

*To make a vegetarian broth, substitute konbu (dried kelp) for dashinomoto. Konbu, also sometimes spelled "kombu," is available at most specialty grocery stores. As a rule of thumb, use a piece of konbu about 1 inch long per 1 c. of water. Wipe any dust or dirt off the pieces with a damp paper towel, but do not rinse under running water. Cut each piece of konbu into thirds and place in a saucepan with the required amount of water. Soak for at least 15 minutes. Add soy sauce and sugar and place over high heat. Just before boiling, carefully remove konbu with a slotted spoon and discard. Follow the rest of the directions for noodles.

Tea / Ocha

Ever since the ninth century A.D., the Japanese have been drinking tea. A filled teapot stands on Japanese tables during every meal. A cup of tea is also often enjoyed during any conversation, business or social. Although the Japanese drink many varieties of tea, loose green Japanese tea is still the most popular. It is always drunk plain, without milk, sugar, or lemon.

loose green Japanese tea

water

1. In a teakettle or saucepan, heat water to boiling and cool for 5 minutes.

2. Measure loose tea into a teapot. Use 1 tbsp. per cup of water.

3. Pour hot water into the teapot and let stand for a few minutes.

4. Pour tea into cups. (Do not add additional water to the teapot until more tea is desired. This preserves the fragrance of the liquid and prevents the tea from becoming bitter.)*

Cooking time: 15 minutes

*Iced mugi cha, or roasted barley tea, is a popular summer drink in Japan. Most specialty grocery stores carry mugi cha, either loose or in tea bags. If loose, use 2 tbsp. barley per 1 c. water and bring to a boil in a teapot. Reduce heat and simmer for about 3 minutes. Strain with a sieve and chill before serving. If using tea bags, follow brewing directions on package.

Soup / Shirumono

Soup is an important part of most Japanese meals. Clear soup (*osumashi*) is usually served at the beginning of a meal. This delicately flavored soup can be varied by the addition of many different kinds of garnishes. The slightly thicker, sweeter soups flavored with red or white soybean paste (*misoshiru*) are generally served toward the end of a formal Japanese meal. Both kinds of soups can be made with dashinomoto, a powdered soup base available at specialty grocery stores.

Basic clear soup (left), eggdrop soup (top), and bean paste soup (right) accompany many Japanese meals. (Recipes on pages 42–43.)

Basic Clear Soup / *Osumashi*

3 c. water

1 heaping tsp. dashinomoto

½ tsp. salt

½ tsp. soy sauce

4 mushroom slices for garnish

chopped chives for garnish

1. In a saucepan, bring water to a boil.

2. Stir in dashinomoto, salt, and soy sauce.

3. Remove immediately from heat. Pour into 4 small bowls and garnish each with a mushroom slice and a pinch of chives.

Preparation time: 10 minutes
Cooking time: 2 minutes
Serves 4

Eggdrop Soup / *Tamago Toji*

1 egg

2 tbsp. scallions, finely chopped

3 c. basic clear soup
(see recipe above)

1. Beat egg and scallions together in a small bowl.

2. In a saucepan, bring basic clear soup to a boil.* Swirl egg mixture around the inside of the pan in a small stream, making a circle.

3. Remove soup from heat and pour into 4 small bowls to serve.

Preparation time: 5 to 10 minutes
Cooking time: 5 to 10 minutes
Serves 4

*Try adding a couple of sliced mushrooms or a few snow peas to this soup for a special taste treat. Simply add the extra veggies to the basic clear soup a minute or two before the boiling point.

Bean Paste Soup/Misoshiru

3 c. water

2 tbsp. dashinomoto

½ c. miso*

½ c. cubed tofu

2 scallions, chopped into thin
 rounds for garnish

1. In a saucepan, bring water to a boil and stir in dashinomoto and miso.

2. Add tofu and bring mixture to a boil again.

3. Remove from heat, pour into 4 small bowls, and garnish with scallions.

Preparation time: 10 to 15 minutes
Cooking time: 10 minutes
Serves 4

*Miso is available in a variety of colors, from creamy
white to red or dark brown. A yellow or golden-colored
miso is the most common and can be used for the recipes
in this book. However, each variety has its own distinct
flavor, and as you continue to explore Japanese cooking
you may want to experiment with different types of miso.

Dishes with Sauces/ Sunomono and Aemono

Sunomono and aemono dishes include vegetables and seafood mixed with various kinds of sauces. The ingredients may be raw or lightly cooked to preserve their natural colors and textures. Sauces for sunomono dishes always include vinegar, while aemono sauces are made from toasted sesame seeds, soy sauce, miso, and many other good things.

When planning a Japanese meal, you might think of sunomono as playing the same role as salads do in an American meal. Their tangy dressings and crisp textures provide a good contrast to meat dishes. Aemono dishes such as *goma-ae* give a special taste to familiar green vegetables like broccoli, green beans, and spinach.

Living in an island nation, the Japanese have ready supplies of fresh seafood. Impress your friends by serving kani to kyuri no sunomono, *or cucumber with crab—a tasty, refreshing dish. (Recipe on page 48.)*

Sesame Seed Dressing with Broccoli / *Goma-ae*

Goma-ae (sesame seed dressing) is served at room temperature, so it can be prepared ahead of time. This dish can be made with broccoli, spinach, green beans, cabbage, cauliflower, or any other fresh green vegetable you have on hand.

1 lb. broccoli, cut into small pieces
   (do not use tough ends of stalks)

3 tbsp. sesame seeds*

3 tbsp. soy sauce

1 tbsp. sugar

1. Bring 6 c. water to a boil in a saucepan. Add broccoli and cook for one minute. (Be careful not to overcook. Broccoli should be bright green when done.) Drain and set aside.

2. Prepare sesame seeds by putting them in a covered, dry frying pan and toasting them over medium heat, shaking the pan constantly so that seeds do not burn. When seeds turn golden brown (about 3 minutes) remove the pan from the heat. Place seeds in a small bowl and crush lightly with the back of a large spoon, or process in a blender for a few seconds.

3. Combine soy sauce, sugar, and sesame seeds and mix well. Toss with broccoli and serve.

*Unless specified, most Japanese recipes use the white variety of sesame seeds. Black sesame seeds have a stronger flavor and are often used as a decorative garnish.

Preparation time: 5 to 10 minutes
Cooking time: 8 to 12 minutes
Serves 4

Cucumber with Crab/*Kani to Kyuri no Sunomono*

This refreshing combination of cucumber slices and crabmeat has a tart dressing made with vinegar. For variety, you could use shrimp or scallops in place of the crab. Or serve the cucumber alone with the sunomono dressing.

2 cucumbers

1 tsp. salt

6 oz. canned crab or frozen crab, thawed

Dressing:

¼ c. rice vinegar

2 tbsp. sugar

¼ tsp. soy sauce

sesame seeds (optional)

1. Thinly slice cucumbers, place in bowl, and sprinkle with salt. Let stand for 5 minutes, then use your hands to gently squeeze water out of cucumbers.

2. Break crab into small pieces.

3. In another bowl, combine vinegar, sugar, and soy sauce.

4. Put cucumber and crab in 4 small bowls and pour on dressing. Sprinkle with sesame seeds, if desired.

Preparation time: 15 minutes
Serves 4

Boiled Spinach/Horenso

Another category of vegetable dishes, ohitashi, is boiled greens served with soy sauce and topped with katsuobushi or toasted sesame seeds.

1 lb. fresh spinach*

3 tbsp. katsuobushi or toasted sesame seeds

2 to 4 tsp. soy sauce, to taste

1. Wash spinach well and cook in steamer or in pan with ½ c. water for about 3 minutes. (Do not overcook. Spinach should be bright green when done.)

2. Drain spinach and set in cold water to stop the cooking process. Then use your hands to squeeze out as much water as possible.

3. Cut spinach into 1- to 2-inch pieces and place in 4 individual bowls.

4. Garnish with katsuobushi or toasted sesame seeds (see page 46 for toasting instructions) and pour soy sauce over spinach.

Preparation time: 5 minutes
Cooking time: 3 to 5 minutes
Serves 4

Other vegetables, such as broccoli or green beans, make tasty substitutions for spinach in this recipe.

One-Pot Dishes/Nabemono

Nabemono dishes combine meat or seafood and vegetables in one pot to make a hearty and satisfying meal. In Japan, "nabe" cooking is done at the table, using a pot heated over a gas or charcoal burner. Meals featuring nabemono are particularly popular in the winter because the heat of the burner warms the room as well as cooks the food.

To make your nabemono dish, you can use an electric frying pan or casserole. If you want to cook at the table as the Japanese do, prepare your ingredients ahead of time and arrange them neatly on a platter. Then invite your family and friends to watch while you cook a delicious *sukiyaki* or *mizutaki*.

Crisp greens and tender chicken make mizutaki *(recipe on page 54) a real treat.*

Simmered Beef and Vegetables / Sukiyaki

Although Japanese diners do not eat beef very often, sukiyaki is one of the most popular and well known of the nabemono dishes, both in Japan and in North America. If you choose to substitute bite-sized pieces of chicken for beef, this dish is called torisuki.

1 to 1½ lb. rib-eye of beef

1 12-oz. block tofu, cut into 1-inch cubes*

1 tbsp. oil

1 bunch (about 6) scallions, cut into 2-inch pieces

1 small can shirataki

1 8-oz. can sliced bamboo shoots, rinsed under cold, running water

1 c. sliced fresh mushrooms

1 c. soy sauce

1½ c. water

3 tbsp. sugar

1. Slice beef very thinly. (If meat is slightly frozen, it is much easier to cut.)

2. Heat oil in frying pan and sauté beef.

3. Add scallions, shirataki, bamboo shoots, mushrooms, and tofu.

4. Combine remaining ingredients to make a sauce. Pour sauce over meat and vegetables until they are half covered. Adjust heat so that sauce simmers.

5. After about 10 minutes, test a piece of meat to see if it is done.

6. Remove from pan and serve with hot rice.

Preparation time: 10 minutes
Cooking time: 30 minutes
Serves 4

*To make delicious and satisfying vegetarian sukiyaki, simply omit the beef from the recipe and double the amount of tofu.

Chicken in a Pot/Mizutaki

This simple chicken dish is served with a dipping sauce that adds a spicy taste. For color or garnish, you might want to add 1 c. of chopped carrots at the same time that you put in the cabbage. A similar dish prepared with beef is called shabu shabu, and when fish is used, it is called chirinabe.

1½- to 2-lb. chicken, in serving
  pieces*

2 c. plus 4 c. water

2 c. Chinese cabbage, chopped

soy sauce

1. Place chicken in cooking pot with 2 c. water and bring to a quick boil. Drain immediately. (If you are cooking at the table, this step should be done ahead of time.)

2. Add 4 c. fresh water and heat to simmering. Simmer for 20 minutes.

3. Add Chinese cabbage and cook for 10 more minutes.

4. Remove chicken and vegetables to individual serving plates. If desired, the remaining liquid may be served as soup. Season to taste with soy sauce.

Preparation time: 10 minutes
Cooking time: 45 to 55 minutes

Dipping Sauce:

½ c. soy sauce

juice of 1 lemon (about 3 tbsp.)

Garnish:

1 tbsp. chopped chives or scallions

½ tbsp. grated ginger root or grated
radish and red pepper, mixed

1. Mix soy sauce and lemon juice and pour into 4 small bowls.

2. Place garnishes in 4 small bowls.

3. Mix sauce and garnish to individual taste.

4. Dip chicken and vegetables in sauce before eating.

Preparation time: 10 minutes
Serves 4

*After handling raw chicken or other poultry, always
remember to thoroughly wash your hands, utensils,
and preparation area with soapy hot water. Also, when
checking chicken for doneness, it's a good idea to cut
it open gently to make sure that the meat is white
(not pink) all the way through.*

Broiled Dishes/Yakimono

Many popular Japanese dishes are prepared by broiling. This method of cooking over high heat makes food crisp on the surface and tender and juicy inside. Meat, seafood, and vegetables are all delicious prepared as yakimono.

In Japan, "yaki" dishes may be cooked at the table on a small charcoal grill called a hibachi. If you don't have a hibachi, then a backyard barbecue grill or the broiler in your oven will work just as well. (When cooking with charcoal, it's a good idea to have an experienced cook help you start the grill.)

(Top) Teriyaki *(recipe on page 58)* and (bottom) kushiyaki *(recipe on page 59)* are both cooked in delicious sauces to add flavor.

Broiled Chicken/ *Teriyaki*

One of the tastiest yakimono dishes is teriyaki, meat or seafood broiled with a sauce that gives it a shiny, glazed coating. This simplified recipe is baked in the oven instead of broiled, as broiled food can burn easily. Beef, pork, shrimp, and some kinds of fish are also delicious prepared with teriyaki sauce.

½ c. soy sauce

3 tbsp. sugar

I tsp. fresh ginger root, grated

3 tbsp. sesame seeds

1½- to 2-lb. chicken, cut into serving pieces

1. Preheat oven to 375°F.

2. Combine soy sauce, sugar, ginger root, and sesame seeds in a large bowl.

3. Place chicken in a baking dish and pour sauce over it. Bake for 45 minutes. Brush on more sauce as chicken bakes (about every 15 minutes).

Preparation time: 15 to 20 minutes
Cooking time: 45 minutes
Serves 4

Broiled Shrimp and Vegetables / *Kushiyaki*

Another popular category of yakimono is kushiyaki, foods broiled on skewers. (Kushi is the Japanese word for "skewer.") Like so many Japanese specialties, kushiyaki can be made with a combination of many different ingredients. Seafood, beef, pork, chicken, and vegetables such as mushrooms, onions, green peppers, and zucchini all make great kushiyaki. Use your imagination and pick your own favorites.

¼ c. soy sauce

2 tbsp. sugar

1 tbsp. fresh ginger root, grated

1 green pepper

1 lb. fresh whole mushrooms

1 lb. large fresh shrimp, peeled and deveined,* or 2 7-oz. packages frozen peeled raw shrimp, thawed

*If you use fresh shrimp for this recipe, you may be able to have it peeled and deveined at the grocery store. Otherwise, you can do it yourself. Hold the shrimp so that the underside is facing you. Starting at the head, use your fingers to peel off the shell from the head toward the tail. Then, using a sharp knife, carefully make a shallow cut all the way down the middle of the back. Hold the shrimp under cold running water to rinse out the dark vein.

1. Combine soy sauce, sugar, and ginger root in a bowl.

2. Clean out and cut green pepper into 1-inch pieces. (Mushrooms may be broiled whole.)

3. Have an experienced cook start the charcoal grill, or preheat the oven to the broil setting.

4. Alternate shrimp, green pepper, and mushrooms on 12 small wooden skewers.

5. Grill or broil skewered shrimp and vegetables for 6 to 10 minutes, or until done. Carefully drizzle or brush sauce over the skewered shrimp and vegetables several times during broiling. Turn the skewers often so that all sides are broiled evenly.

6. Pour remaining sauce over skewers and serve with hot rice.

Preparation time: 10 to 15 minutes
Cooking time: 6 to 12 minutes
Serves 4

Salt-Broiled Fish / *Shioyaki*

Salt broiling is a simple but delicious way to prepare fish. The salt sprinkled on the fish before broiling gives it a special flavor. Any small whole fish may be cooked in this way. Fillets, or boneless pieces of fish, may also be used as long as the skin is left on.

2 whole trout, cleaned, or 1 lb. fish
    fillets with skin on

salt

soy sauce

lemon wedges

1. Salt fish lightly on both sides and leave at room temperature for 30 minutes.

2. With help from an experienced cook, start charcoal grill or preheat broiler.

3. Grill or broil fish for about 5 minutes on each side or until golden brown.

4. Serve with soy sauce and lemon wedges.*

Preparation time: 35 minutes
Cooking time: 10 to 15 minutes
Serves 4

*Grated daikon (Japanese white radish) adds a bit of extra zip to a dipping sauce for shioyaki. Give each diner a small dish to mix soy sauce, lemon, and daikon to his or her personal taste.

Simple flavors and ingredients help this fish dish shine.

Holiday and Festival Food

Japanese cooks prepare all meals carefully and with great attention to attractive presentation. Holidays and festival meals are no exception. In fact, since these dishes are for special occasions, it is even more important that they look and taste wonderful. They may contain more ingredients than ordinary recipes, and some dishes call for unusual or specialty items. Certain foods have special meaning or symbolism, while others are chosen for their color or appearance.

All of these factors can make holiday and festival dishes a bit more challenging to prepare than everyday fare. However, Japanese cooks feel that the results are well worth the extra effort. When you try these recipes yourself, remember that this is food for celebration. Have fun making it, and have fun eating it with family and friends!

Ozoni (recipe on page 64) is traditionally served on New Year's.

Rice Cake Soup with Shrimp/*Ozoni*

Ozoni is the traditional Japanese New Year's soup. The recipe for ozoni varies from region to region, but it always contains mochi (glutinous rice cakes) and usually has vegetables or greens and some kind of meat or fish. Though some Japanese cooks still make their own mochi, many now purchase them already prepared. In the United States, mochi are available at most specialty grocery stores.*

4 dried shiitake mushrooms

1½ c. warm water

pinch of sugar

3 c. basic clear soup, without mushrooms or chives (see recipe on page 42)

4 jumbo shrimp (fresh or frozen), peeled and deveined

12 to 16 leaves of fresh spinach, rinsed

4 mochi

4 thin strips of lemon peel for garnish (optional)

1. Soak dried shiitake mushrooms for about 20 minutes in 1½ c. warm water with a pinch of sugar. Remove from water and set the water aside. (Do not discard.) Cut off mushroom stems and rinse mushrooms under cold water. Squeeze mushrooms as dry as you can, cut each one in half, and place them in a saucepan.

2. Add 1 c. of the water you set aside to the saucepan. Add basic clear soup and bring mixture to a simmer. Cover and cook for 12 to 15 minutes.

3. While soup is simmering, cook shrimp in boiling water for 2 to 3 minutes. Remove from heat, drain, and set aside.

4. In a small saucepan, barely cook spinach leaves in boiling water for 30 to 40 seconds. The leaves should just begin to wilt. Drain, rinse leaves under cold water, and drain again. Squeeze water out of the leaves and set aside.

5. Soak mochi in a saucepan of warm water for 5 minutes, then bring water to a boil. Cook for 1 minute or until they begin to soften. Drain and put each mochi in a small bowl. Place one shrimp and 3 or 4 spinach leaves on each mochi. Add 2 mushroom halves to each bowl. If desired, add a strip of lemon peel as a garnish.

6. Remove the soup from heat and pour into the 4 bowls. Serve immediately.

Preparation time: 45 minutes
Cooking time: 15 to 20 minutes
Serves 4

*Shrimp is a popular ingredient in New Year's dishes such as ozoni, since the shrimp's bent back symbolizes old age and long life.

"Scattered" Sushi Rice/ *Chirashi-zushi*

In addition to the traditional sweets eaten on Hina Matsuri (Girls' Day), chirashi-zushi has become a popular dish for girls and their friends to share at their doll-viewing tea parties.

2 c. short-grain white rice, uncooked

2 ⅓ c. water

4½ tbsp. rice vinegar

½ tbsp. sugar

½ tbsp. salt

vegetable oil

4 dried shiitake mushrooms

1½ c. warm water

1 small carrot, peeled and cut into thin sticks

1½ tbsp. soy sauce

1½ tbsp. sugar

3 tbsp. lemon juice

10 oz. canned crabmeat, or frozen crab, thawed

½ c. green peas, fresh or frozen

2 eggs

½ tsp. sugar

pinch of salt

1. Wash rice in a pan with cold water until water is clear. Drain and place rice in a covered heavy pot or saucepan with 2⅓ c. water. Soak for 1 hour.

2. Bring rice and water to a boil. Lower heat and simmer until water is absorbed (about 25 minutes). Turn off heat and let sit for 10 minutes. Remove rice from pot and place in a large serving bowl.

3. While rice is cooking, mix rice vinegar, sugar, and salt in a small bowl until sugar and salt dissolve. Sprinkle mixture over rice and gently fold it into the rice with a wooden spoon or spatula. Leave to cool.

4. Soak shiitake in 1½ c. warm water for 30 minutes. Remove from water and set water aside. Cut off mushroom stems and squeeze mushrooms dry. Cut into thin shreds.

5. In a small saucepan, combine ½ c. of mushroom-soaking liquid, soy sauce, 1½ tbsp. sugar, mushrooms, and carrot sticks. Cover and bring to a boil. Remove lid and simmer for 2 minutes, stirring constantly. Remove from heat, drain, and set aside.

6. Sprinkle lemon juice over crabmeat and let sit for 5 minutes. Squeeze extra liquid out of crabmeat, break into small pieces, and set aside.

7. Boil green peas until they are tender. Remove from heat, drain, and set aside.

8. Beat eggs with ½ tsp. sugar and pinch of salt. Heat a frying pan lightly coated with vegetable oil and pour in half of egg mixture, tilting pan to make a thin omelet. Fry over low heat for 30 seconds or until surface of omelet is dry. Carefully remove omelet with a spatula and place on a cutting board. Repeat with remaining mixture. When omelets are cool enough to handle, cut into thin strips.

This festive dish is easy to adapt to your personal tastes. Omit the eggs and the crabmeat to create a tasty vegetarian entrée. Or, you can add almost any veggie you like to the mix—be creative!

9. With a wooden spoon or spatula, fold about half of the mushrooms, carrot, peas, and crabmeat into the rice. Scatter the remainder, along with omelet strips, on top and serve at room temperature.

Preparation time: 1½ to 2 hours
Cooking time: 1 hour
Serves 4 to 6

Noodle Soup with Chicken and Bean Paste/
Miso Ramen

Although ramen noodles are originally from China, they are very popular in Japan, and Japanese cooks have created many of their own unique ramen dishes. Miso ramen was first made in Sapporo, a northern city famous for its Snow Festival and its many ramen shops.

¼ lb. chicken breast*

9 oz. ramen noodles, instant or fresh-dried

5 c. chicken or vegetable broth

1 1-inch piece of fresh ginger root, crushed

6 tbsp. miso

1½ tbsp. soy sauce

salt and pepper to taste

2 scallions, chopped into thin rounds

1. Place chicken breast in a large saucepan with enough water to cover. Bring to a boil. Turn heat to low, cover pan, and simmer for 30 minutes. Carefully remove chicken to a small bowl or plate to cool.

2. While chicken is simmering, cook ramen noodles in 6 c. boiling water until they soften, about 2½ to 3 minutes for instant and 5 to 6 minutes for fresh-dried. Drain and rinse with cold water. Divide noodles among four bowls. When chicken is cool enough to handle, use your fingers to shred it into thin strips and divide strips among the four bowls, on top of the noodles.

3. In a saucepan, combine chicken or vegetable broth and ginger root and bring to a simmer. Simmer for 10 minutes. Use a slotted spoon to carefully remove and discard ginger. Keep broth over low to medium heat.

4. In a small bowl, combine miso and a small amount of the heated broth. Mix well and add to saucepan. Add soy sauce and salt and pepper to taste.

5. Pour hot broth into bowls. Garnish with scallion rounds and serve.

Preparation time: 10 minutes
Cooking time: 45 to 55 minutes
Serves 4

*Instead of chicken, try adding spinach leaves, mushrooms, or bean sprouts to this flavorful broth. Just barely cook spinach in boiling water for 30 to 40 seconds, or lightly stir-fry mushrooms or bean sprouts in a little vegetable oil.

Index

About the Author

Reiko Weston came to Minneapolis, Minnesota, from Tokyo, Japan, in 1953. She studied math at the University of Minnesota but interrupted her studies in 1959 to open a Japanese restaurant called Fuji-Ya in downtown Minneapolis. Fuji-Ya has changed locations several times, but continues to be a popular eating place.

Weston was named Small Businessperson of the Year in 1979. In 1980, she became the second woman to be elected to the Minnesota Hall of Fame. Ms. Weston played an active role in managing her restaurant until her death in 1988.

Photo Acknowledgments: The photographs in this book are reproduced courtesy of: © David Samuel Robbins/Corbis, pp. 2–3; © Walter, Louiseann Pietrowicz/September 8th Stock, pp. 4 (left), 5 (both), 6, 20, 32, 35, 40, 44, 47, 50, 53, 56, 61, 62; © Robert L. & Diane Wolfe, pp. 4 (right), 39; © Robert Holms/Corbis, p. 11; Cameramann International, Ltd., p. 12; © AFP/Corbis, p. 13; © Michael S. Yamashita/Corbis, pp. 15, 17; Charles Gupton/Stone, p. 28.

Cover photos: © Robert L. & Diane Wolfe, front top; © Walter, Louiseann Pietrowicz/September 8th Stock, front bottom, spine, and back.

The illustrations on pages 7, 21, 29, 31, 33, 34, 37, 38, 41, 42, 43, 45, 46, 49, 51, 52, 55, 57, 60, 63, 65, 67, and 69 and the map on page 8 are by Tim Seeley.